D0787157

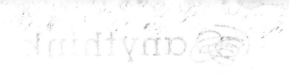

DO YOU REALLY WANT TO MEET STEGOSAURUS?

BY ANNETTE BAY PIMENTEL • ILLUSTRATED BY DANIELE FABBRI

AMICUS ILLUSTRATED and AMICUS INK
are published by Amicus
P.O. Box 1329, Mankato, MN 56002
www.amicuspublishing.us

EDITOR: Rebecca Glaser
DESIGNER: Kathleen Petelinsek

LIBRARY OF CONGRESS CATALOGING-IN-PUBLICATION DATA
Names: Pimentel, Annette Bay. | Fabbri, Daniele, 1978-
    illustrator.
Title: Do you really want to meet stegosaurus? / by Annette
    Bay Pimentel ; illustrated by Daniele Fabbri.
Description: Mankato, Minnesota : Amicus, [2018] | Series: Do
    you really want to meet a dinosaur? | Audience: K to grade 3.
Identifiers: LCCN 2016044431 (print) | LCCN 2016045011 (ebook)
    | ISBN 9781681511146 (library binding) | ISBN 9781681521398
    (pbk.) | ISBN 9781681512044 (e-book) | ISBN 9781681512044
    (pdf)
Subjects: LCSH: Stegosaurus—Juvenile literature. |
    Dinosaurs—Juvenile literature.
Classification: LCC QE862.065 P56 2018 (print) | LCC QE862.
    065 (ebook) | DDC 567.915/3--dc23
LC record available at https://lccn.loc.gov/2016044431

Printed in the United States of America
HC 10 9 8 7 6 5 4 3 2
PB 10 9 8 7 6 5 4 3 2 1

ABOUT THE AUTHOR
Annette Bay Pimentel lives in Moscow, Idaho with her family. She doesn't have a time machine, so she researches the past at the library. She writes about what happened a long time ago in nonfiction picture books like *Mountain Chef* (2016, Charlesbridge). You can visit her online at www.annettebaypimentel.com.

ABOUT THE ILLUSTRATOR
Daniele Fabbri was born in Ravenna, Italy, in 1978. He graduated from Istituto Europeo di Design in Milan, Italy, and started his career as a cartoon animator, storyboarder, and background designer for animated series. He has worked as a freelance illustrator since 2003, collaborating with advertising agencies and international publishers, including many books for Amicus.

You and Max sport your own style. No wonder Stegosaurus is your favorite dinosaur! Too bad it's extinct. Wouldn't it be great to watch Stegosaurus in action?

You'll need a time machine.
To find a living Stegosaurus,
you'll need to go back 153 million
years to the Jurassic Period.
Bring extra water and food—
there are no kitchens! But where
do you need to go? Try Colorado.
Lots of Stegosaurus fossils
have been found there.

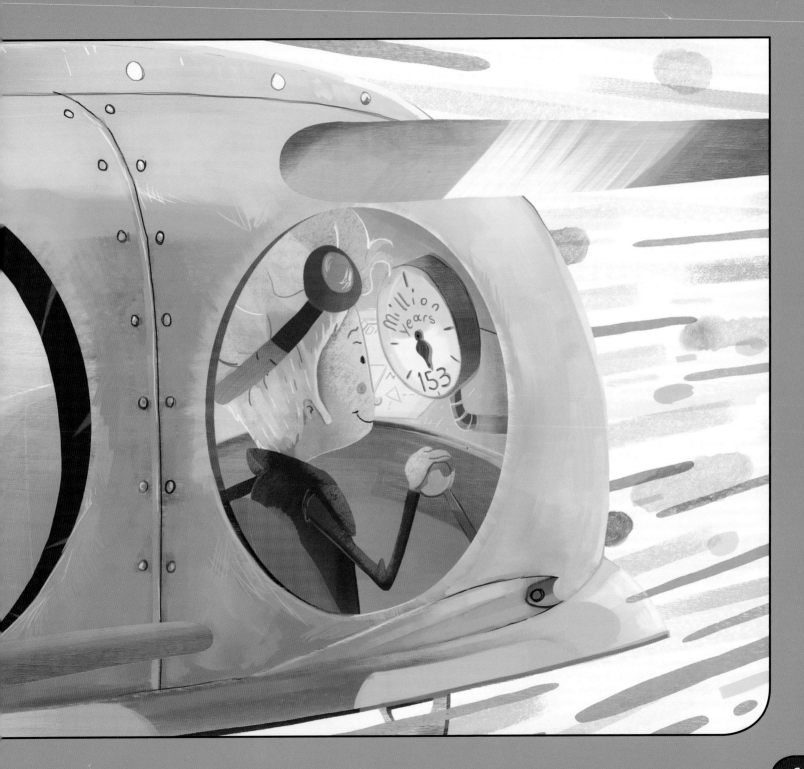

Is this Colorado? Yes. There were no mountains here 153 million years ago. It's hot, dry, and wide-open flat land, like a savanna.

Max loves sniffing around the ferns. Maybe he smells dinosaur. Your nose isn't that good, but you see a dinosaur. It's a meat-eating Allosaurus on the hunt! Lay low until it passes.

Look at the watering hole. There's a whole herd of Stegosauruses!

Each adult is almost the size of a school bus.

But they're not all big. The younger ones are the size of a car.

All of them have bony plates on their backs.

Why do they have plates on their backs? Scientists aren't sure.

Maybe the plates help the Stegosaurus cool off.

They probably help one Stegosaurus recognize another. Just like your hairstyle helps everyone know it's you!

You're hungry. The Stegosauruses are eating, too. They use their beaks to yank leaves off plants. They chew with their small teeth. They're herbivores, but they won't steal your carrot. It's too thick. They can only bite through leaves and soft stems.

Stegosaurus babies! You didn't notice them from a distance. They're so little! One weighs about the same as an average newborn human baby, 6.5 pounds (3 kg).

Can you see their tiny tracks? Each footprint is the size of a quarter.

Oh no! Allosaurus is heading straight for the Stegosauruses!

Look at its sharp teeth! Most of the Stegosauruses tramp away...

But one big Stegosaurus turns its side to the Allosaurus. It swings its tail. Thwack! Big spikes on its tail make contact. The Allosaurus stumbles backwards, bleeding. It runs away. The big Stegosaurus lumbers back to the herd.

Time to leave. If you could stay longer, you'd try to solve the mystery of the Stegosaurus plates. You'd watch their babies grow up. But right now, you and Max need to get home for dinner.

WHERE HAVE STEGOSAURUS FOSSILS BEEN FOUND?

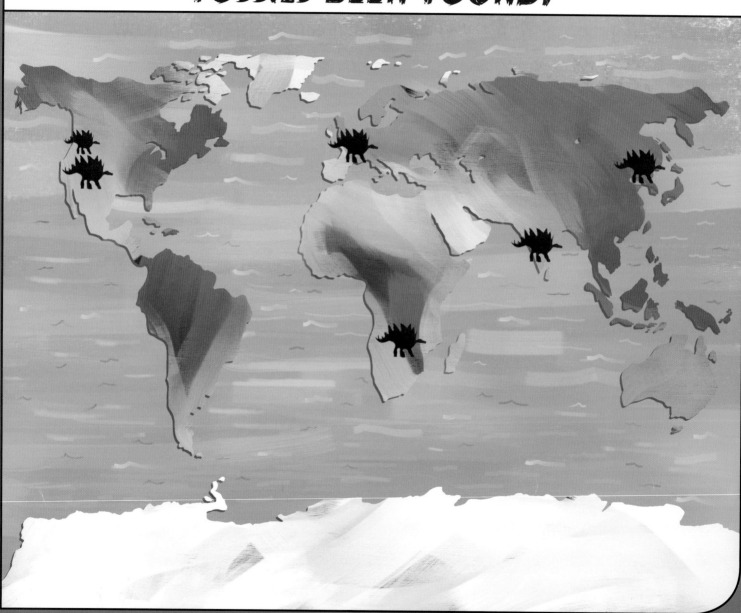

GLOSSARY

Allosaurus—A large meat-eating dinosaur.

extinct—No longer found living anywhere in the world; known only from fossils.

fern—A plant with feathery leaves and no flowers; it is one of the oldest kinds of plants on Earth.

herbivore—An animal that eats only plants.

herd—A group of animals that live and travel together.

Jurassic Period—The time period from 200 million to 145.5 million years ago, when Stegosaurus and other dinosaurs lived.

savanna—A flat, grassy plain with few or no trees.

AUTHOR'S NOTE

Too bad for us, time machines aren't real. But the details about Stegosaurus in this book are based on research by scientists who study fossils. In 2005, scientists announced they had studied an Allosaurus bone with a hole in it—and the hole matched the shape of a Stegosaurus tail spike. This suggests that Stegosaurus used its tail to fight Allosaurus. New dinosaur discoveries are made every year. Look up the books and websites below to learn more.

READ MORE

Alpert, Barbara. *Stegosaurus*. Mankato, Minn.: Amicus, 2014.

Holtz, Thomas R. *Digging for Stegosaurus*. North Mankato, Minn.: Capstone Press, 2015.

WEBSITES

DINOSAURS: DISCOVERY KIDS
http://discoverykids.com/category/dinosaurs/
Play games, watch videos, and try online activities to learn more about these fascinating extinct animals.

DINOSAURS: NATIONAL GEOGRAPHIC KIDS
http://kids.nationalgeographic.com/explore /nature/dinosaurs/
Compare sizes of dinosaurs, meet paleontologists, and more.

Every effort has been made to ensure that these websites are appropriate for children. However, because of the nature of the Internet, it is impossible to guarantee that these sites will remain active indefinitely or that their contents will not be altered.